#RockYourBook On a Global Scale To Grow
your Business/Build Relationships

10 Ways to Market Your Book Like A ROCK STAR!

ROCK YOUR Book

Bestselling Author & Marketing Coach

La' Tanyha Boyd

ROCK YOUR BOOK: 10 Ways to Market Your
Book like a Rockstar

Copyright © 2016 by LÁ TANYHA BOYD

ISBN: ISBN-13: 978-1540307231

Cover & Interior Design: TamikaINK.com

Printed in USA

ABOUT THE AUTHOR

Là Tanyha, is also the leading Marketeer in leveraging ministries and brands across the globe as #RockYourBook Virtual Tours is one of the top existing Virtual Book Tours business. Helping emerging authors and national bestsellers to create and Rock their brand/message/books on a global scale that will attract profits.

Là Tanyha has been coined as the Book Marketing Coach Mid-Wife or Book Marketing Godmother to many indie & International Bestselling Author's in achieving their literary goals and gain media exposure.

Là Tanyha's passion is to engage, and inspire the multitudes and to win souls across the globe through the airways, her writings, and speaking engagements while empowering others to move forward in this journey called LIFE.

Note from the Author: Reviews are gold to authors! If you've enjoyed this book, would you consider rating it and reviewing it on
Amazon's Author's
La Tanyha Boyd Page:
amazon.com/author/latanyhaboyd

OTHER BOOKS BY LA'TANYHA BOYD

People Eat with their Eyes: How to Create an Effective Book Trailer
ISBN-13: 978-1500182199
http://amzn.com/B00L9FXSJK

People Eat with Their eyes and a book trailer (video) captivates people and draws them in. FINALLY A BOOK TO TEACH YOU: How to capture the attention of your reader with a book trailer, How to design your own book trailer on a shoestring budget, How to use the book trailer to launch a marketing campaign with your book

OTHER BOOKS BY LA'TANYHA BOYD

Jumpstart Your Day: 31 Inspirational Quotes
ISBN-13: 978-1491264393
http://amzn.com/B00EWLNVXQ

Learn how to Jump Start Your Day and line up your thoughts, desires and emotions with the Word of God. 'Spiritual Food for Thought: 31 Inspirational Quotes to Jump-Start your Day,' is a daily devotional, consists of inspirational messages that offer daily words of empowerment, and promote spiritual growth and development in the Lord Jesus Christ for your day to day living.

OTHER BOOKS BY LA'TANYHA BOYD

FAITH LEARNS THE POWER OF PRAYER

ISBN-13: 978-1501077784

http://amzn.com/B00NR4REFA

"Faith: Learns The Power Of Prayer" is a book that emphasizes the importance of putting the Lord in whatever step you take. The book says that there is no where the Lord cannot hear your prayers, it's all about believing and taking the right actions. This book says faith comes by hearing and hearing of the words of the Lord and most importantly understanding what the Lord is communicating to you.

#RockYourBook w/3C's To Building your Author's
Platform RT @LaTBoyd1 #MarketingBookCoach

https://youtu.be/vwgu0IkZ-dQ

TABLE OF CONTENTS

Learn How to Build Your Online Author's Platform

Why not maximize your reach beyond the group of friends, & the handful family members on Facebook, or the couple of followers on Twitter and those few blog readers; and begin to reach hundreds and thousands of people globally today!

A platform is the thing you have to stand on to get heard and to be seen. It's your stage! Unlike a stage at a concert hall, today's platform is built of people, contacts, connections, followers, influencers and supporters.

As an author, it's important to invest time and energy into building your platform: establishing relationships, and gain potential readers.

Just like standing on a stage and having all eyes on you. A strong author platform can lift you above the competition and

give you a much better chance of success and gaining all-eyes-on-you.

In the past, platform-building happened in the physical world. It involved speaking at events, sending out mailings, handing out business cards and networking at events with fellow writers and so on.

As networking has evolved, I found that the online world is a wonderful tool to create an online presence, build your author's platform and establish business relationships.

Here are four key ways you can do just that:

Key #1: Blog-It!

If you haven't yet established an online presence, the best way to begin is with a blog. This gives you a "home base" on the web that you can fill with whatever content you want. Here are a fee WordPress.com, Blogspot.com Squarespace, Weebly and Wordpress.org. You can set up a blog completely for free here, or you can buy a unique domain name.

What should you blog about? That's up to you, but most bloggers find it easiest to build an audience when they **"stick to what they know."** Keep in mind a blog does not have to be long. I've found that a short blurb of inspiration with a photo to be very effective.

Or

- ❖ **Writing and writing advice** – this can work well if you're looking for writing/editing work.
- ❖ **Almost any topic (cooking / technology / fashion)** – this is great for non-fiction writers specializing in a particular area.
- ❖ **Fiction-centered** – if you've written a novel, your blog could tie in with the fictional world, perhaps offering short stories or excerpts from the book.

Key #2: You Got Mail!

An email list is a great next step after a blog. The huge advantage of an email list is that it gives you direct access to your audience. For most people, email is a comfortable and familiar technology, and they'll probably see every email from you – whereas they might only visit your blog occasionally.

While you can allow readers to subscribe to your blog by email, you may well want to create a separate email newsletter through a service like Aweber or MailChimp. (MailChimp is free at the basic level.) Madmimi (offers a free option), as does Getresponse.

Your newsletter could be:

- ❖ **Short tips and advice for your clients and potential clients** – plus an occasional special offer, or announcement of a new service.
- ❖ **A regular short article related to your blog topic** – you could also include links to some of your best recent blog posts.
- ❖ **A monthly update about your next novel-in-progress** – along with a gentle reminder to buy the current one (or to tell a friend).

Key #3: Let's Get Social!

Social media is a great way to reach new people and grow your platform. It shouldn't be your only platform-building focus, though. You're limited by the constraints of different sites (e.g. a tweet can only be 140 characters) and often, only a fairly small proportion of your audience will see any given tweet or Facebook update.

There are dozens of different social media sites, some of the most popular ones are:

➢ Facebook
➢ Twitter
➢ LinkedIn
➢ Google+
➢ Pinterest
➢ Instagram (Image driven)
➢ Snapchat (allows fun behind the scenes look at your business

- ➢ Periscope (Live Broadcast
- ➢ Youtube
- ➢ Facebook Live (allows for live facebook broadcasts...it is a separate app download though)

Totally understand how having so many social media platforms can be overwhelming. I recommend that you invest your energy in one or two social networks, rather than trying to be present on half-a-dozen: think about where your ideal customer or ideal reader is likely to be. For me, Facebook is a great place to keep readers up-to-date, and Twitter is a great place to build relationships with fellow writers and bloggers.

Staying ultra-connected and active can get daunting after a while. Try Linking your Facebook account with your Twitter account this will make it even easier for you to share updates in one place globally.

Key #4:
Let's Get Organized!

Set up an editorial calendar. This not only aids in organization, but can increase your productivity and decrease overwhelm. As ideas come up, you can add them to the calendar, move things around and notice "holes" in your content.

Try scheduling automated post(s) and manage multiple networks and profiles with one step and enhance your social media platforms. Facebook has this option; as does Hootsuite.

Other scheduling platforms:

Hootsuite (free option, pro version $14.99)
MeetEdgar $50 per month (continuously recycles info)
Buffer $10/Month
Co-Schedule (works great with blogs...wordpress.org)
EClincher begins at $10 per month (like meet edgar)

IFTTT gives you creative control over the products and apps you love.

Key #5:
In It For the Long Haul-
Consistency...

Creating an Online Presence is crucial for any business; however being '**consistent**' with your message creates brand recognition and helps reinforce the quality of your brand. These networks/platforms are the most effective and cost efficient tools to help enhance the visibility of your brand. One of the most important aspects of social media is to be social! Create and publish content regularly that others will enjoy and share with their friends online. It's important to make sure your content is relevant to your industry, brand, and customers in order for your brand recognition to increase.

Key #6:
Monetize Social Media Engagement

Schedule social media. Decide when and what you will share on your social media platforms. Optimize your profile on Twitter, Facebook, Google+, LinkedIn, Goodreads and Pinterest. Select the most effective time for reaching the most people with Tweriod, Sprout Social or Buffer.

Get a professional and distinctive author photo. Use this image across all your social media profiles, on your site, at the end of your book (along with your author bio) and on your print materials.

Tell your author brand story. Write an author biography that succinctly defines your reason for being; keep it to two or three short but memorable paragraphs that will resonate with your readers. Show some personality and give your readers a reason to care.

Key #7:
Build Your Author Brand

But Wait! I'm sure you're asking yourself what exactly does "branding" mean? Your brand is your PROMISE to your audience.

It tells them what they can expect from you and your work, and it differentiates what you have to offer from that of your competitors. **Your brand stems from who you are, how you want to be known and who people perceive you to be**. Branding is how we market ourselves to others, and the best way to do so is by discovering and revealing who we are on the inside.

We all have a personal brand because we are always being judged, assessed and evaluated by others. By conscientiously building your author brand, you can do several things:

- You can enhance your writing by giving it greater focus and depth

- You can cultivate the tone, texture and phrasing of your work–refine your voice

- You can control–to a degree–how you and your work are perceived (it's up to you what face you want to show the world, but I do recommend you show the real one)

- You can make it easier for readers to identify your books or work in a crowded marketplace

- You can attract new readers that identify with your brand

- You can even create change, start a movement, or lead by example

Branding has become more about serving others, and by doing so, your sphere of influence and visibility increases. Authenticity and transparency too, are key to building trust and community with your audience.

And although the web can amplify an author's visibility, building your brand takes a lot of time, energy and determination. The reward for all this effort? Empowerment, confidence and a network of loyal fans.

A solid launch of your new writer's brand is very important; don't hurry and don't be sloppy. This is a good reason why you don't want to wait to have your book deal in hand before you begin building your author platform. Having to hurriedly piece something together will only end in disappointment – for you and your potential readers.

Take the time you need to best represent your brand. However, also keep in mind that perfection isn't possible. Put your best work forward, but understand that it is a work in progress. Over time it will be your audience's feedback and comments that help "perfect" your brand.

Design your author website, business cards, bio, author photo, cover design and print materials with your brand or message in mind. Be concise and consistent. Remember that colors, **fonts and other imagery should all add to the story, not detract from it**. Make sure your logo graphically represents and unifies your message and develop a tagline that quickly conveys what you do and differentiates you from the competition.

#RockYourBook w/3C's To Building your Author's Platform RT @LaTBoyd1 #MarketingBookCoach

https://youtu.be/vwgu0IkZ-dQ

Key #8:
Create Book Buzz

Now that you have refined your brand personality and taken the time toward solidifying and polishing your concept, it's time to live your message and incorporate it into all of your plans for the future.

Develop exceptional pre-launch content. Craft posts that are core to your message and are indicative of the kinds of things you'll be writing about in the future.

Guest post frequently and strategically. Guest blogging is one *the* best ways to increase visibility, gain influence in your genre or topic and draw targeted readers to your online 'bookstore' or author site.

Link your book to trending topics. Write articles that tie your book topic or genre to current popular interests.

Create a press release. A good press release will include the information needed for a reporter or blogger to understand the news value of your story. Make sure it's clear what you are announcing, why the reader of the press release should care, and where they can get more info if they're interested. Then submit your press release to

Develop exceptional pre-launch content. Craft posts that are core to your message and are indicative of the kinds of things you'll be writing about in the future.

Key #9:
Capture the Attention of Your Reader with a Book Trailer

People Eat with Their Eyes. A book trailer (video) captivates people and draws them in. Having a Video Book Trailer for your book will provide you with opportunities to connect with your audience and sell more books!

Book trailers are a great marketing tool and is quickly gaining popularity among publishers and successful authors to help promote books and encourage people to read them. Bestsellers have them – why not you? Introduce your book and get potential readers excited!

From Wikipedia, the free encyclopedia:
A **book trailer** is a <u>video</u> advertisement for a <u>book</u> which employs techniques similar to those of <u>movie trailers</u> to promote books and encourage

readers.[1] These trailers can also be referred to as "video-podcasts", with higher quality trailers being called "cinematic book trailers".[2] They are circulated on television and online in most common digital video formats.[3] Common formats of book trailers include actors performing scenes from the book akin to a movie trailer, full production trailers, flash videos, animation or simple still photos set to music with text conveying the story.[4] This differs from author readings and interviews, which consist of video footage of the author narrating a portion of their writing or being interviewed.[5] Early book trailers consisted mostly of still images of the book, with some videos incorporating actors

Online book trailers can be effective tools for marketing and gaining potential readers. With that said book marketing efforts need to be ***productive*** not just ***active***.

Your book trailer allows potential readers to see the essence of your novel or non-fiction book in an entertaining short film. The aim of an effective book trailer would say YES to the following questions:

- Did it grab your attention?
- Do you want to share it with someone?
- Do you want to watch it again?
- Where you moved (touched with emotions)?
- Most importantly, are you going to check out the book now?

Online book trailers can be an effective tool for book marketing as well as creating book buzz for an upcoming release. With more and more video production tools becoming accessible and easy to use, you might think about using an online book trailer to promote your book. Here's how to get started laying out your book trailer.

Your book trailer can have a compelling effect; when well produced and marketed. A book trailer is a video advertisement for a book which employs techniques similar to those of a movie trailer. Just like an effective movie trailer, you want too, convey that same essence for your book without giving too much away.

Book trailers are a great marketing tool and is quickly gaining popularity among publishers and successful authors to help promote books and encourage people to read them. Bestsellers have them – why not you? Introduce your book and get potential readers excited!

People Eat With Their Eyes: How To Create An Effective Book Trailer
by La'Tanyha Boyd
Link: http://amzn.com/B00L9FXSJK

FINALLY A BOOK TO TEACH YOU:

· How to capture the attention of your reader with a book trailer
· How to design your own book trailer on a shoestring budget
· How to use the book trailer to launch a marketing campaign with your book

Key #10:
Rock Your Book Launch

Build your email list. Invite people to subscribe, and make it worth their while by providing remarkable content. Use your list wisely to create and build buzz for your launch. Engage your tribe early, keep them 'in-the-loop', and ask for feedback so they become invested in the successful outcome of your book or project.

Launch week promotion. Leverage social media by letting your followers know of your launch date and providing progress updates. Try and schedule a guest post for launch week to drive more people to your new site.

Launch day and beyond. Make sure your launch day content is unmistakably great. Consider a press release, a special sale, promo or offering your prospective audience something for free. Connect and respond to your new visitors and try and form a bond to keep them coming back for more.

Make it easy to buy. Ensure your author website includes book links that are clear, easy to find, and go directly to your listing at every retailer you're listed with (Amazon, Smashwords, B & N, Kobo, or Apple iBookstore).

The launch of your website and brand is a big—and usually one time—event. So take advantage.

Bonus #1
Rock Your Book Radio Interview

Preparation and practice will build your confidence and help you get great coverage.

1. Know how much time you will have. A five minute segment will limit the number of opportunities you have to convey your central points. A 20 minute interview will allow time for 3 or 4 stories to illustrate your point.

2. Decide what points you want to get across during the interview, and drive them home at the outset. Why? If you go into an interview with no idea what you want to say the host may steer it to a totally different topic.

3. Use the questions you are asked as an opportunity to quickly pivot off a short answer and circle back to your principle

talking points. Mention the name of your book every 90 seconds.

4. Study the style of your host. Listen to interviews they have conducted with other personalities. Do they let their guests talk absent interruption? Do they pepper the guest with questions? Do they allow the guest to control the interview or do they try to veer the topic to something the host wants to discuss?

Practice Makes Perfect:
Rehearse Out loud in front of a mirror, into a tape recorder or video camera, or to a friend – this will help you feel prepared and build your confidence.

➢   Don't just be ready to make your plug, be ready to talk AT LENGTH. Assume the interviewer knows NOTHING about you, your background service or product.

➢   Be significant in some way. Stick out. Be distinctive. (Have a signature story, an outrageous claim) that gets you remembered.

➢ Know your social media links and purchase product links.

➢ Don't be afraid to mention any upcoming speaking events you'll be participating in. i.e. conferences, telesummit, etc.

Good Business:

It's never a bad idea to thank the host, commentator or journalist for the interview– it will be appreciated.

Bonus #2:
Secret Sauce: Rock Your Book on Amazon

Reach More Readers Create your Amazon.com Author Page

At Author Central, you can share the most up-to-date information about yourself and your works with millions of readers. Visit my page: amazon.com/author/latanyhaboyd

Add your biography, photos, blog, video, and tour events to the Author Page, your homepage on Amazon.com. https://authorcentral.amazon.com/

ABOUT THE AUTHOR

Rock Your Book With Marketing Coach Lá Tanyha Boyd

Branding/Promotions/Marketing Expert |CelebrityPR| 4x's Bestselling Author | International Talk-Show Host iWorship96FM Radio

LàTanyha, has over 20 years of outstanding expertise in Strategic Marketing, Leadership, Social Media Marketing/Branding and Self-Publishing coupled with Book Marketing Coaching. As the President of You're your Faith Tours Branding/ Promotions/ Marketing Co. she has initiated creative marketing, branding and communication solutions for non-profit organizations, small business, indie/self-publish authors and corporations.

LáTanyha Boyd, is a high energy, Empowerment Coach, Transformation Strategist, Bestselling Author, and

Branding/Promotions/Marketing expert. She is living her dream and walking in her calling to empower, inspire others in "Living in the Now," the abundant life.

LàTanyha, has penned her Fourth Best Selling book '**Rock Your Book: 10 Ways to Market Your Book Like a Rock Star**!' She is gifted and prolific Best Selling Author of her very first book **"Spiritual Food for Thought: 31 Inspirational Quotes to Jump Start Your Day!"** And her Second Bestseller **People Eat With Their Eyes: How to Create an Effective Book Trailer.** Author Boyd, continues to use the ***power of the pen*** with her third Bestselling release and first Children's Christian Fiction Short-Story entitled: **"Faith: Learns The Power Of Prayer."** LàTanyha, has lend her voice with a powerful **Audio teaching entitled: "Change That Stinkin-Thinking."**

In the industry Là Tanyha, has been coined as the Marketing Book Coach/Branding Mid-Wife/Godmother to many Indie & Best-Selling Author's in achieving their literary goals. She continues to excel in her role as a Publicist to many Indie & Best-Selling Author's and business owners in establishing an online presence; Build Author
platform, Establish relationships, and Grow their business Globally.

Are you ready to Turn-Up your Social Media Engagement? Jump start your Marketing Plan OR Brand like a RockStar? Book Your Coaching Session with Marketing Coach LàTBoyd - Helping Emerging businesses, ministries, authors and national bestsellers to create and Rock their brand/message on a global scale that will Grow Your Business and Build Relationships...

Visit:
http://bit.ly/MarketingCoachLaTBoyd

Sign up for our next #RockYourBook Trainings and Interviews
http://bit.ly/RockYourBook

Note From Author: Reviews are gold to authors! If you've enjoyed this book, and found great value would you consider rating it and reviewing it on Amazon's Là Tanyha Author's Page amazon.com/author/latanyhaboyd

LA'TANYHA BOYD

LA'TANYHA BOYD

www.ingramcontent.com/pod-product-compliance
Lightning Source LLC
Chambersburg PA
CBHW061227180526
45170CB00003B/1193